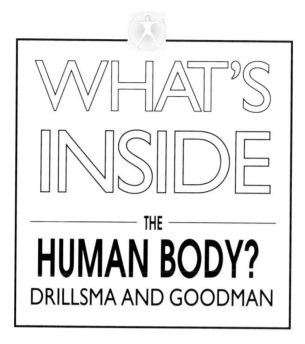

WHAT'S INSIDE

THE
HUMAN BODY?

DRILLSMA AND GOODMAN

PETER BEDRICK BOOKS

NEW YORK

Published by
PETER BEDRICK BOOKS
2112 Broadway
New York, NY 10023

Published by agreement with
Wayland Publishers, England

Library of Congress Cataloging-in-Publication Data
Drillsma, Barbara
    What's inside the human body? / Barbara Drillsma,
Sally Goodman. –
    – 1st American ed.
    p.   cm.   — (What's inside?)
Includes index.
Summary: Presents an illustrated survey of the functions and
anatomy of the human body.
    ISBN 0-87226-398-3
    1. Human physiology-—Juvenile literature. 2. Human
anatomy--Juvenile literature. [1. Human physiology. 2. Human
anatomy. 3. Body, Human.] I. Goodman, Sally, 1966–
II. Title. III. Series: What's inside? (Peter Bedrick Books)
QP37.D75   1997
612--dc21   97–23416
                                                                       CIP
                                                                        AC

First American edition 1997
Printed in Hong Kong

Commissioning Editor: Thomas Keegan
Designer: John Kelly
Editor: Nicky Barber
Illustrators: Oxford Illustrators and the Maltings Partnership
Typesetters: Dorchester Typesetting Group Limited

Contents

Introduction

The body is like a huge factory with thousands of workers in different departments. All these workers depend upon each other to keep the body running efficiently. This whole process is controlled by the operations center, the brain. The brain sends our messages through millions of cables, or **nerves**, to the various departments of the body. A lost message can result in illness.

YOUR BLOOD SUPPLY

The body holds about 1.5 gallons of blood. It travels in a figure eight pattern along the main blood vessels, called **arteries** and **veins**, and the smaller blood vessels, called **capillaries**.

Lungs

Heart

Artery
Vein

Capillaries

PROTECTIVE SKIN

The outer covering of the body, skin, is the body's largest organ. It protects the body from injury, keeps fluids in, and stops harmful substances from entering.

Liver
Pancreas
Digestive system
Large intestine

Stomach

Small intestine

Respiratory system

Trachea

Lungs

Kidneys

Bladder

INSIDE YOUR BODY

The digestive system is tucked neatly inside the body, and is protected by the ribcage. It is made up of a stomach, large and small intestines, pancreas, liver and two kidneys. The kidneys are connected to your bladder. The respiratory system has two large balloon-shaped lungs. The lungs are attached by two bronchi to a windpipe, or trachea, which connects the lungs to the mouth and nose.

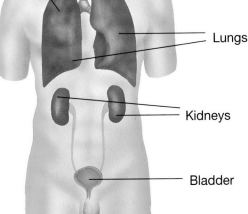

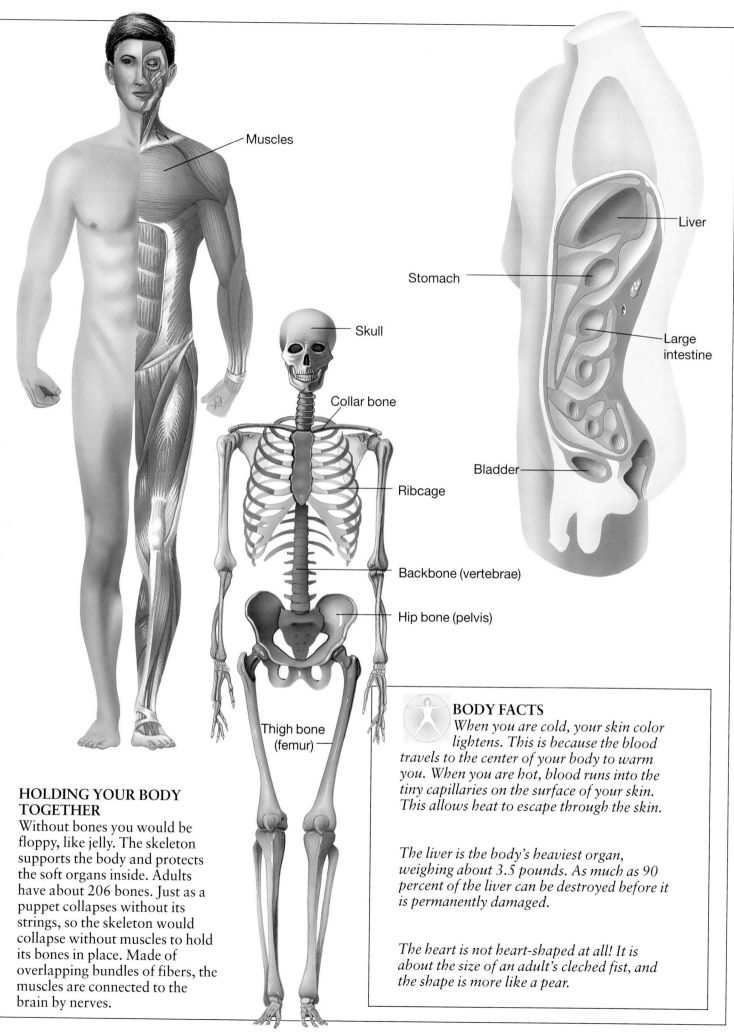

Muscles

Liver

Stomach

Large intestine

Skull

Bladder

Collar bone

Ribcage

Backbone (vertebrae)

Hip bone (pelvis)

Thigh bone (femur)

HOLDING YOUR BODY TOGETHER

Without bones you would be floppy, like jelly. The skeleton supports the body and protects the soft organs inside. Adults have about 206 bones. Just as a puppet collapses without its strings, so the skeleton would collapse without muscles to hold its bones in place. Made of overlapping bundles of fibers, the muscles are connected to the brain by nerves.

BODY FACTS

When you are cold, your skin color lightens. This is because the blood travels to the center of your body to warm you. When you are hot, blood runs into the tiny capillaries on the surface of your skin. This allows heat to escape through the skin.

The liver is the body's heaviest organ, weighing about 3.5 pounds. As much as 90 percent of the liver can be destroyed before it is permanently damaged.

The heart is not heart-shaped at all! It is about the size of an adult's cleched fist, and the shape is more like a pear.

The human cell

The cell is the basic building block of the body. Cells make up all living **organisms** (except for **viruses**). You can imagine a cell as one factory in an industrial park full of factories. Each factory has its own control center – the nucleus – and can work on its own. However, when the factory works together with the others, its efficiency increases. Cells multiply by dividing in two. They continue to divide as long as extra tissue is needed.

LOOKING AT CELLS

It is estimated that there are 75 million, million, millions cells in the adult body. Different cells have different shapes, sizes and structures. The red cells that give blood its color are flat and round, like frisbees. They float along in the bloodstream. Skin cells look like wooden building blocks. Nerve cells are long and thin, ideal for passing messages from the brain and to other nerve cells.

The nucleus is the cell's command and control center. It is surrounded by a protective wall, called a **membrane**. It contains **DNA**, the material that holds your **genetic code**.

Proteins travel through the tiny folded sacs of the Golgi complex to be stored until they are ready for dispatch from the cell.

The endoplasmic reticulum is a maze of channels in the cytoplasm of the cell. It enables all the different parts of the cell to communicate with each other.

The mitochondria contain special chemicals, called **enzymes**. They control the reactions that release energy to the rest of the cell.

The cell membrane is a thin wall that holds the cell together. Substances can pass through the cell membrane on their way in and out of the cell.

Outside the nucleus is a jelly-like substance, called cytoplasm. This contains little spaces, or vacoules, which transport **proteins** and waste material.

Ribosomes make proteins from parts sent from the nucleus. They are tiny and round. Ribosomes are attached to the endoplasmic reticulum (*see below*).

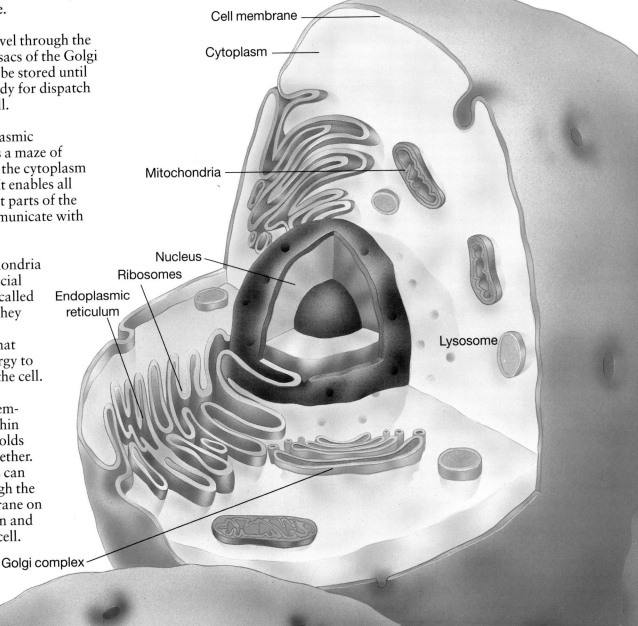

Cell membrane

Cytoplasm

Mitochondria

Nucleus

Ribosomes

Endoplasmic reticulum

Lysosome

Golgi complex

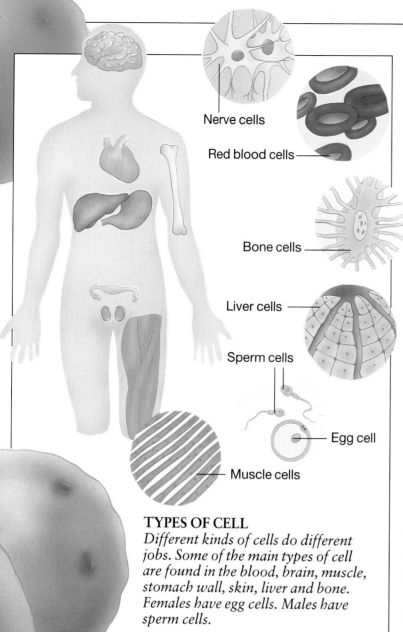

Nerve cells

Red blood cells

Bone cells

Liver cells

Sperm cells

Egg cell

Muscle cells

TYPES OF CELL
Different kinds of cells do different jobs. Some of the main types of cell are found in the blood, brain, muscle, stomach wall, skin, liver and bone. Females have egg cells. Males have sperm cells.

CELL FACTS
Cells have varying life spans. The cells in your nerves can last a lifetime. Bone cells live between 10 and 30 years; red blood cells for four months, and skin cells for seven days.

The biggest cell in the female body is the egg cell, which can just be seen by the human eye. It measures one tenth of a millimeter acorss, the size of a tiny speck of dust.

Unlike other cells, the smallest cell, the red blood cell, has no nucleus. This is because its only function is to carry oxygen. It measures seven thousandths of a millimeter across.

INSIDE THE NUCLEUS
The information that programs your body is stored in the nucleus of each cell on a long ribbon of deoxyribonucleic acid (DNA). The DNA contains all the information needed for your body to grow. When a cell divides, the DNA unravels like a zipper. Two new DNA molecules are formed, one for each new cell.

WHAT IS YOUR BODY MADE OF?
Much of your body is made of water – at least 70 percent! The rest is made up of protein, fat, bone and carbohydrates with tiny amounts of nucleic acid and vitamins.

Digesting your food

The food you eat provides fuel for all the activities carried out by the body. Every process, from the division of cells to the twitching of your nose, requires **energy** that comes from food. But first the food has to be broken down so that it can be absorbed by the body. This is the job of the digestive system.

IN THE MOUTH

As the teeth grind and mash, saliva is poured on to moisturize and soften the food. Saliva is produced in two salivary glands above and below the tongue. Saliva contains an enzyme which helps to break down carbohydrates in food into more easily digestible sugars. The tongue rolls the food around the mouth, forcing it into a soft ball, or bolus, ready for swallowing.

Bolus of food

Muscles squeeze in

PUSHING THE FOOD DOWN

Food is pushed down the esophagus by a process called peristalsis. Muscles in the wall of the esophagus squeeze together to push the bolus of food down to the stomach.

Imagine how uncomfortable it would be if the bolus of food was forced down a dry, rough tube. To prevent this happening, tiny mucous glands line the esophagus and produce a substance that keeps the tube moist.

Mucous glands

Muscles in the esophagus wall

Teeth

Jawbone

Salivary glands

Epiglottis

Trachea

Esophagus

THE ESOPHAGUS

The esophagus begins at the back of the throat and continues down behind the trachea (windpipe) to the stomach. To stop food going down your windpipe there is a flap of skin joined to the larynx, called the epiglottis. When you swallow, the epiglottis prevents food from entering the trachea.

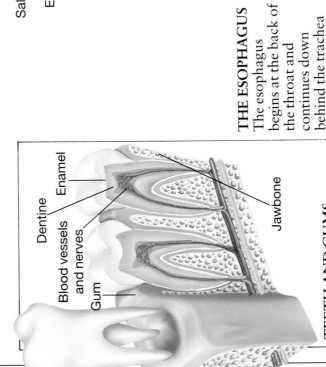

Dentine

Enamel

Blood vessels and nerves

Gum

Jawbone

TEETH AND GUMS

There are 32 permanent teeth for cutting and grinding food. Inside a tooth is a sensitive pulp containing nerves and blood vessels, surrounded by bone dentine. Teeth are coated with a protective, tough covering, called enamel.

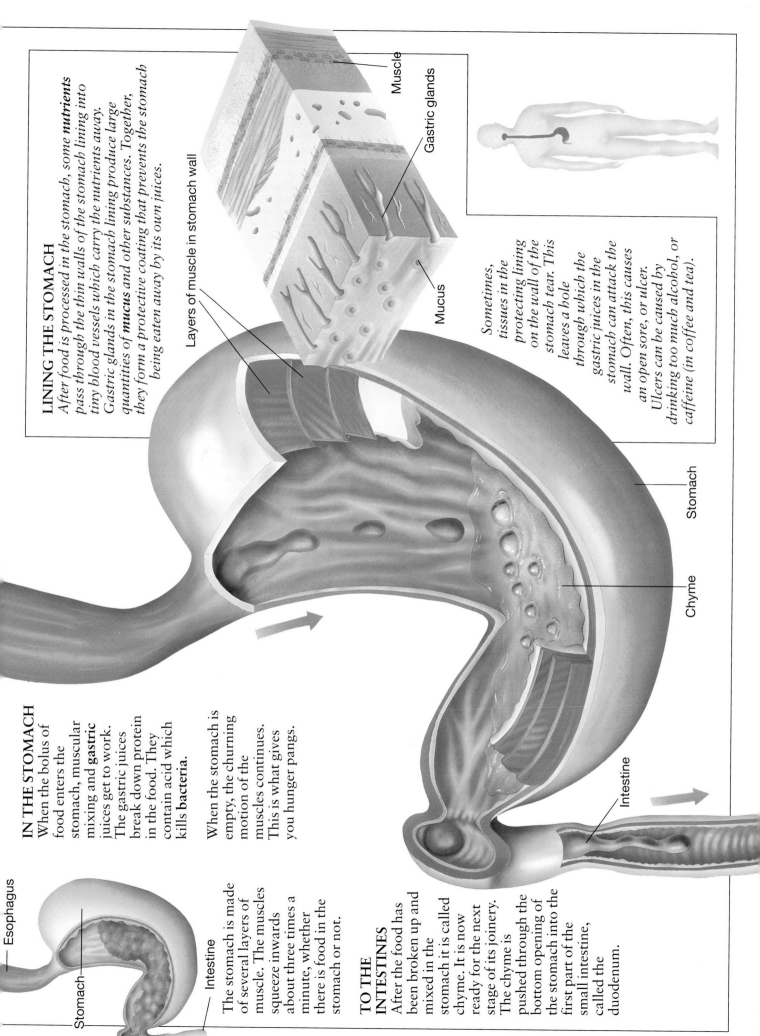

LINING THE STOMACH

*After food is processed in the stomach, some **nutrients** pass through the thin walls of the stomach lining into tiny blood vessels which carry the nutrients away. Gastric glands in the stomach lining produce large quantities of **mucus** and other substances. Together, they form a protective coating that prevents the stomach being eaten away by its own juices.*

Muscle

Gastric glands

Layers of muscle in stomach wall

Mucus

Stomach

Chyme

Intestine

Sometimes, tissues in the protecting lining on the wall of the stomach tear. This leaves a hole through which the gastric juices in the stomach can attack the wall. Often, this causes an open sore, or ulcer. Ulcers can be caused by drinking too much alcohol, or caffeine (in coffee and tea).

IN THE STOMACH

When the bolus of food enters the stomach, muscular mixing and **gastric** juices get to work. The gastric juices break down protein in the food. They contain acid which kills **bacteria.**

When the stomach is empty, the churning motion of the muscles continues. This is what gives you hunger pangs.

The stomach is made of several layers of muscle. The muscles squeeze inwards about three times a minute, whether there is food in the stomach or not.

TO THE INTESTINES

After the food has been broken up and mixed in the stomach it is called chyme. It is now ready for the next stage of its journey. The chyme is pushed through the bottom opening of the stomach into the first part of the small intestine, called the duodenum.

Esophagus

Stomach

Intestine

The end of the journey

The small intestine is made up of the duodenum, jejunum and ileum. It is here that the main work of digestion is carried out. Enzymes from the pancreas and the gall bladder are mixed with the food in the small intestine. As the food is digested, nutrients pass through the walls of the intestine and are carried away in the blood. Waste products move into the large intestine where water is removed before the waste leaves the body.

THE GALL BLADDER

The gall bladder is a small pouch connected to the bile duct. It is used to store bile as it moves from the liver into the small intestine. Bile is a bitter-tasting, greenish-yellow liquid that helps with the digestion of fat.

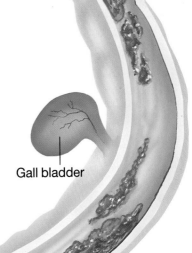

Gall bladder

Pancreas

FOOD BREAKDOWN

The breakdown of food in the digestive system is carried out by 17 enzymes. The enzymes break the food down into small particles that can be absorbed through the walls of the intestine.

THE PANCREAS

The pancreas produces pancreatic juice which helps to digest proteins, carbohydrates and fats. The pancreatic juice moves through the pancreatic duct to the duodenum.

Jejunum

Nutrients absorbed through intestine wall

Small intestine

One villus

Capillaries

Villi

Lymph vessel

The wall of the intestine is not smooth but is covered in many tiny, finger-like projections called villi. The villi increase the surface area of the wall of the intestine, making absorption of digested food easier and more efficient. The villi contain tiny blood vessels, called capillaries, and a **lymph** vessel. Most of the digested food is absorbed by the capillaries, but fats are absorbed by the lymph vessel. Each villus is about one millimeter long. In the ileum, there are about 40 villi on every square millimeter of the wall.

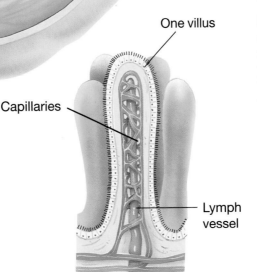

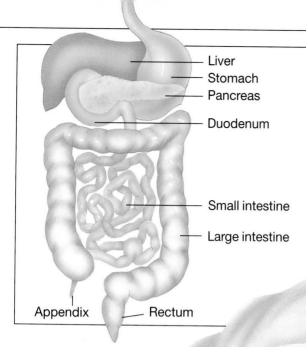

Liver
Stomach
Pancreas
Duodenum

Small intestine

Large intestine

Appendix — Rectum

THE DIGESTIVE TRACT
From the mouth to the anus, the food moves through your digestive tract. At the end of the large intestine is a small tube called the appendix. In rodents, the appendix is used to help digest tough plant food. But in humans the appendix has no job. If it becomes inflamed it has to be removed.

LEAVING THE BODY
After all the goodness has been taken out of the food, the waste is left in the rectum. The waste also contains bacteria, dead cells from the gut lining, and bile **pigments**. The waste leaves the body as feces through the rectum.

Rectum

FOOD FACTS
The food that you eat provides nutrients which are absorbed into the blood. Throughout your body, the cells use the nutrients for different jobs – for repairing, tissues, for growing, to make energy so that the muscles can work, and to protect against disease. Different foods contain different nutrients, so it is

important that you eat a balanced diet which will give you a mixture of all the nutrients you need. Some of the main nutrients are:

*Carbohydrates provide energy. Starch and **glucose** (sugar) are both carbohydrates. They are found in cereals, vegetables, sweets, jam and milk.*

Lipids also provide

energy as well as helping with growth, and forming skin fat to insulate the body and keep heat in. Lipids are found in fats such as butter and margarine as well as nuts and seeds.

*Proteins are made up of **amino acids**. Proteins are essential for growth, and for repairing muscle, bone and skin. Proteins are*

also used inside cells (see page 10). Protein is found in meat, fish, eggs, bread, cereals, potatoes and many other foods.

You eat vitamins in both animal and plant foods. You only need small amounts of vitamins every day. But a shortage of certain vitamins can cause diseases such as scurvy or rickets.

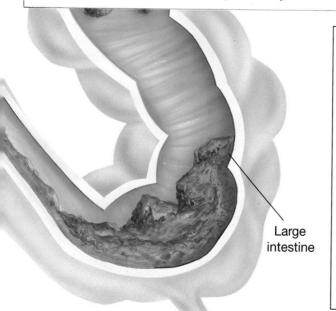

Large intestine

DIGESTION FACTS
The small intestine is longer than the large intestine. The small intestine is about 23 feet long, the largest intestine is about 6 feet long.

Food in the stomach can take between three and six hours to be turned into slushy chyme. Then it can take another hour for the food to reach the intestines. The overall trip through the intestines can taken between eight and 24 hours.

Sometimes people get indigestion – discomfort in the stomach after eating. Often this happens if people eat too quickly. The stomach produces to much acid, causing an uncomfortable feeling.

Liver and kidneys

The largest and heaviest organ in the body is the liver. It lies on the right side just under the lungs and below the diaphragm. It is well supplied with blood vessels. The liver is connected to the heart by the hepatic artery. It also has another blood-carrying supply that comes from the intestine, the portal vein. The liver is the only organ in the body with a blood vein running through it that does not come from, or go directly to, the heart.

THE LIVER

The liver is supplied with blood full of nutrients through the portal vein. It processes the nutrients in the blood, breaking down alcohol and harmful poisons. It turns chemical waste into bile (*see page 14*). It also controls the amount of sugar, called glucose, in the blood.

Another of the liver's many functions is storage. If there is too much glucose in the blood, the liver removes some of it and stores it as glycogen. The liver also stores iron, and some vitamins (*see page 15*).

The liver is a mass of cells and blood vessels. Bile is taken from the liver to the gall bladder through tubes called bile ducts. The liver is divided into two hales, or **lobes**.

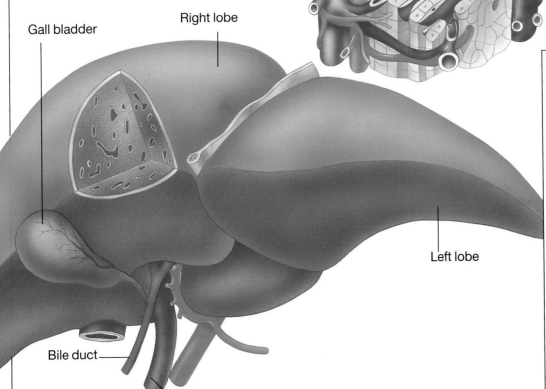

Gall bladder

Right lobe

Left lobe

Bile duct

Portal vein

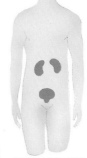

THE URINARY SYSTEM
The urinary system is made up of a pair of kidneys, and two thin tubes called ureters that carry urine to a large bag in which the urine collects, called the bladder.

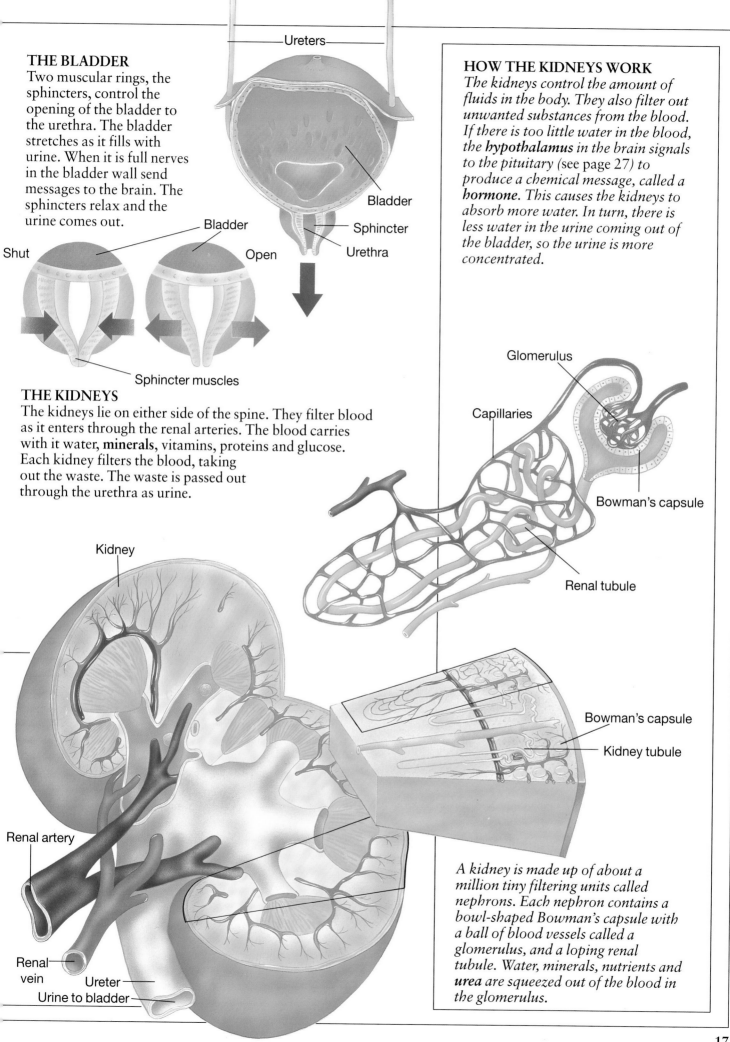

THE BLADDER

Two muscular rings, the sphincters, control the opening of the bladder to the urethra. The bladder stretches as it fills with urine. When it is full nerves in the bladder wall send messages to the brain. The sphincters relax and the urine comes out.

Ureters

Bladder

Sphincter

Urethra

Shut

Bladder

Open

Sphincter muscles

THE KIDNEYS

The kidneys lie on either side of the spine. They filter blood as it enters through the renal arteries. The blood carries with it water, **minerals**, vitamins, proteins and glucose. Each kidney filters the blood, taking out the waste. The waste is passed out through the urethra as urine.

Kidney

Renal artery

Renal vein

Ureter

Urine to bladder

HOW THE KIDNEYS WORK

The kidneys control the amount of fluids in the body. They also filter out unwanted substances from the blood. If there is too little water in the blood, the **hypothalamus** *in the brain signals to the pituitary (see page 27) to produce a chemical message, called a* **hormone**. *This causes the kidneys to absorb more water. In turn, there is less water in the urine coming out of the bladder, so the urine is more concentrated.*

Glomerulus

Capillaries

Bowman's capsule

Renal tubule

Bowman's capsule

Kidney tubule

A kidney is made up of about a million tiny filtering units called nephrons. Each nephron contains a bowl-shaped Bowman's capsule with a ball of blood vessels called a glomerulus, and a loping renal tubule. Water, minerals, nutrients and **urea** *are squeezed out of the blood in the glomerulus.*

Your transport system

Blood, and the transportation system that carries it, is one of the many systems that control the functions of your body. Blood connects every part of the body with every other part. It is a fast and efficient transportation service carrying substances that keep the body alive and healthy. By the time you are an adult you will contain about a gallon and a half of blood. Most of this is water, but the water contains lots of dissolved substances and cells.

BLOOD CLOTTING
Blood contains chemicals that usually prevent it from thickening, or clotting, so that it can flow smoothly. But when you cut yourself, clotting chemicals make the blood produce a protein, called fibrin. This sticks to clumps of platelets and blocks up the hole.

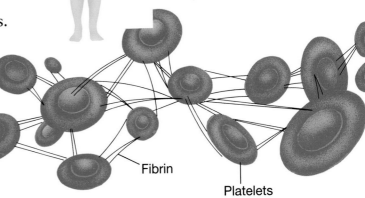

Fibrin

Platelets

WHAT'S IN BLOOD
Blood is made up of a liquid called plasma which contains lots of water and dissolved substances. Blood also contains living cells and fragments of cells called platelets. Red blood cells transport oxygen and white blood cells fight disease.

BLOOD FACTS
Some people, usuall men, inherit a disease called hemophilia. These people do not have one of the chemicals needed to make the blood clot. If they cut themselves the blood clots very slowly, and sometimes not at all. They bleed very seriously.

There are four types of blood. The four blood groups are called A, B, O, and AB. If you need extra blood from someone else, doctors will make sure you get blood which is the same, or compatible with, your own blood group.

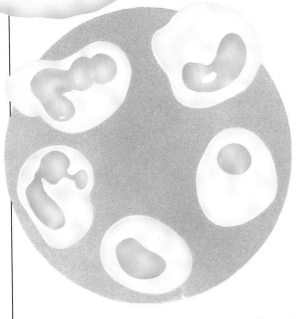

*There are five types of white blood cells. They are all involved in fighting disease. Some of them can actually leave the blood system and squeeze through tiny spaces in the tissue to reach the area of infection. There, they surround the germs and destroy them. Some white cells produce **antibodies** which protect the body from further infection by the same germ.*

Hemoglobin

THE COLOR OF BLOOD
Red blood cells have a large surface area to allow oxygen and carbon dioxide to enter and leave the cells easily. Inside are large amounts of protein called **hemoglobin**. Oxygen combines with the hemoglobin to make oxyhemoglobin, which is a bright red color. The oxygen makes a weak link so that it can detach itself easily when it reaches the body cells where it is needed. The blood traveling back to the lungs has lost its oxyhemoglobin, so it looks purplish in color.

Blood is pumped round the body in two different systems. One system carries blood from the heart to the lungs, and black again. The other system carries blood from the heart all around the body.

The fresh oxygen-rich blood is carried from the heart in the largest artery in the body, called the aorta. This splits into other major arteries. One carries blood upwards to the head and arms. Another artery branches off to take blood to the stomach, liver and intestines. This artery branches again to take blood down to the legs, kidneys and genitals

The veins return blood carrying the waste products and carbon dioxide produced by the cells to the heart. Veins usually run next to the arteries.

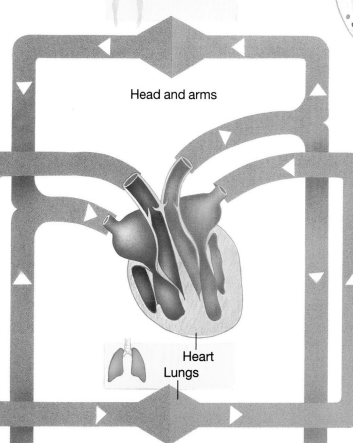

Head and arms

Heart
Lungs

Liver

Stomach
and
intestine

Kidneys, genitals
and legs

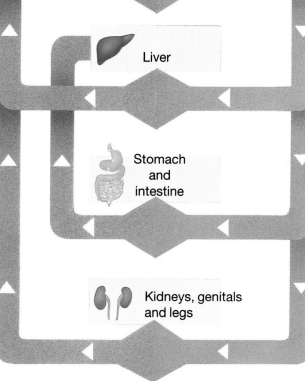

Artery

ARTERIES
Arteries are strong, elastic vessels with thick walls that carry blood away from the heart. The walls contain lots of elastic and muscle tissue. This gives them enough strength and flexibility to withstand the pressure caused by the pumping action of the heart.

Vein

CAPILLARIES
Capillaries are the smallest blood vessels in the body. They form a massive network of tiny tubes connecting arteries with the veins, so that blood can flow continuously around the body.

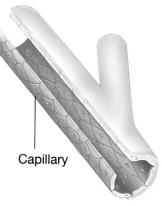

Capillary

VEINS
Veins carry blood towards the heart. The walls of veins are thinner and contain less muscle and elastic tissue than arteries because the blood returning to the heart is not under such high pressure.

The heart pump

Blood needs to be pumped around the body at a constant pressure so that it can flow uphill and downhill at the same rate. The heart is a hollow pump about the same size as your fist. It lies between your lungs and rests on a sheet of muscle called the diaphragm. It pumps blood around the body providing food and oxygen for the cells, and carrying waste products away from the cells.

The heart is divided into four separate parts, called chambers, with muscular walls. The two upper chambers are called the left and right atria, and the two lower chambers are called the right and left ventricles. Blood enters the heart from the lungs and body through veins into the atria. It is then pumped through valves to the ventricles, and out through arteries.

YOUR BEATING HEART
The right atrium receives blood from the body cells through two large veins called the vena cava. The left atrium receives oxygen-rich blood from the lungs through the pulmonary veins.

When the atria contract (squeeze together) blood is forced through the valves into the ventricles. The squeezing action of the heart is controlled automatically by a special nerve center in the heart. When the ventricles contract, oxygen-rich blood leaves the left ventricle through the aorta, the largest artery in the body. The right ventricle sends blood through the pulmonary arteries back to the lungs to receive more oxygen.

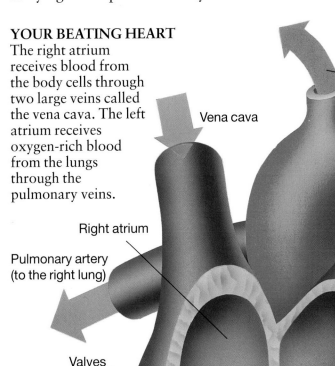

Aorta

Vena cava

Right atrium

Pulmonary artery (to the right lung)

Valves

Pulmonary artery (to left lung)

Pulmonary veins

Left atrium

Right venticle

Vena cava

Left ventricle

HEART TISSUE
The heart is made up of several layers. The outer layer is a protective layer of fatty tissue. The thick middle layer is made of special muscle cells which can all contract at once. The inside layer makes the heart elastic.

Valves

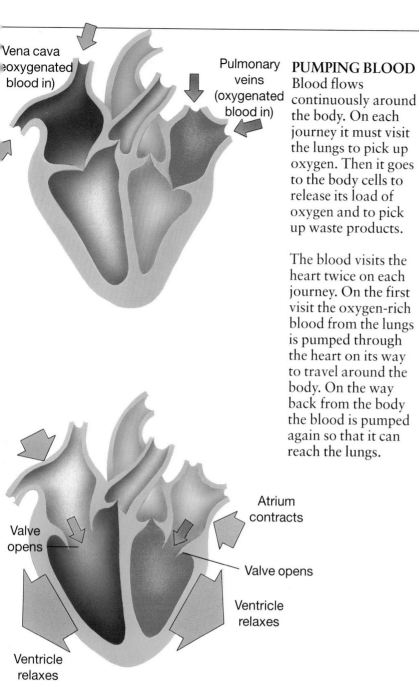

Vena cava (deoxygenated blood in)

Pulmonary veins (oxgenated blood in)

PUMPING BLOOD

Blood flows continuously around the body. On each journey it must visit the lungs to pick up oxygen. Then it goes to the body cells to release its load of oxygen and to pick up waste products.

The blood visits the heart twice on each journey. On the first visit the oxygen-rich blood from the lungs is pumped through the heart on its way to travel around the body. On the way back from the body the blood is pumped again so that it can reach the lungs.

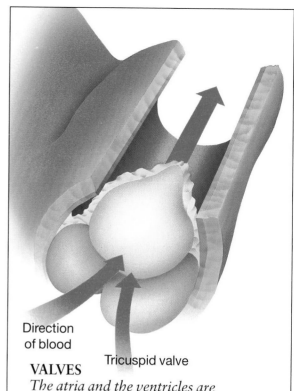

Direction of blood

Tricuspid valve

VALVES

The atria and the ventricles are separated by valves which allow blood to flow in one direction only. The valves have two (bicuspid) or three (tricuspid) flaps held in place by strong fibers. There are also valves at the bottom of the ventricles to stop blood flowing back into the heart. The flaps open and close rhythmically as the heart contracts.

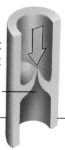

Valve open

Valve shut to prevent blood running back

Valve opens

Atrium contracts

Valve opens

Ventricle relaxes

Ventricle relaxes

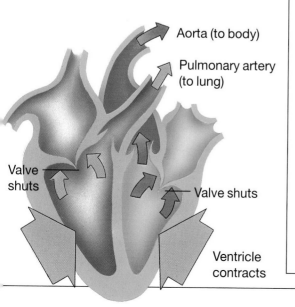

Aorta (to body)

Pulmonary artery (to lung)

Valve shuts

Valve shuts

Ventricle contracts

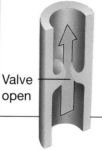

HEART FACTS

A heart attack occurs when one portion of the heart stops working, usually because of a blood clot in an artery. The body will die if starved of oxygen-rich blood for more than a few minutes.

The first heart transplant was carried out in South Africa by Dr. Christian Barnard in 1967.

Your heart will beat about 70 times a minute for the rest of your life. That's about 3 billion times over an average lifespan.

Heard through a stethoscope, your heart beat has a 'lub-dub' sound. This is the sound made by the aortic and pulmonary valves stopping blood flowing back into the heart.

Breathing in and out

Breathing brings oxygen from outside into your body. The air containing the oxygen is cleaned and warmed by the nose before it reaches the lungs. Inside the lungs, the oxygen is brought close to the blood supply that will carry it around the body. Breathing out allows the body to get rid of waste gases such as carbon dioxide and **water vapor**. Breathing is controlled automatically by the body's nervous.

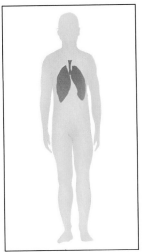

INTO YOUR NOSE

Air enters your body through your nose and mouth. The nose is warm, wet and hairy. The tiny hairs help to clean the air of any dust particles. Behind the nostrils the nose opens out into a large hollow cavity with a lining that produces a wet, sticky mucus. This mucus also traps dust. The warmed air passes from the nasal cavity and down the throat to the larynx. A small flap called the epiglottis stops food passing down this tube.

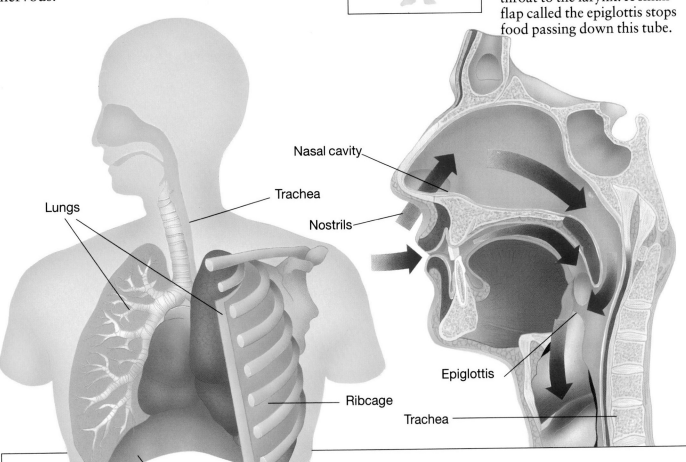

Lungs

Trachea

Nasal cavity

Nostrils

Epiglottis

Ribcage

Trachea

Diaphragm

THE DIAPHRAGM MUSCLE

The diaphragm is a large dome-shaped sheet of muscle sitting just below the lungs. When the muscle contracts, the diaphragm moves downwards, making a bigger space around the lungs. Air rushes in from outside to fill the lungs up. When you breathe out the diaphragm muscle relaxes and moves upwards, making a smaller space around the lungs. This forces air out of the lungs.

As the diaphragm moves downwards, the space around the lungs gets larger and air rushes into the lungs.

Contracts

When the diaphragm moves upwards, the space around the lungs gets smaller again and air is forced out of the lungs.

Relaxes

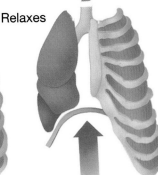

Diaphragm

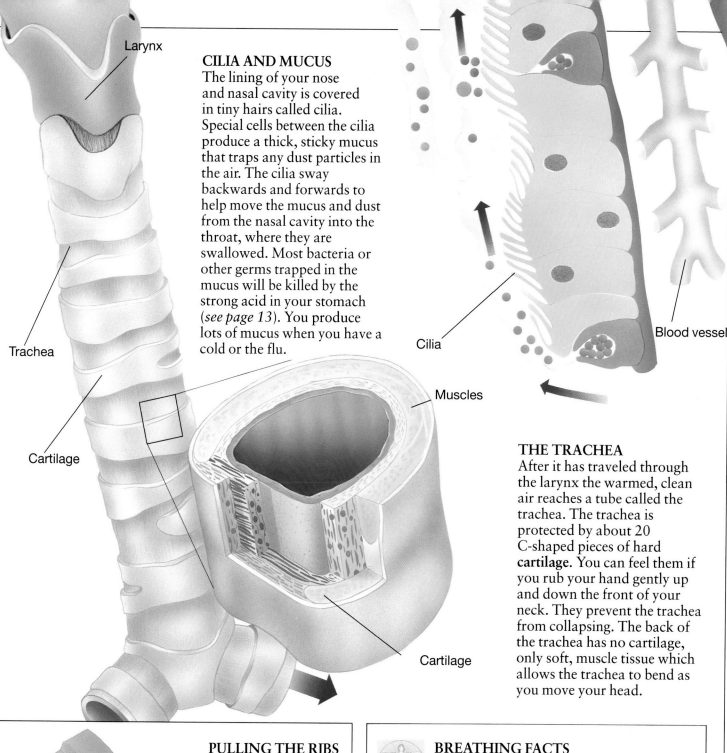

CILIA AND MUCUS
The lining of your nose and nasal cavity is covered in tiny hairs called cilia. Special cells between the cilia produce a thick, sticky mucus that traps any dust particles in the air. The cilia sway backwards and forwards to help move the mucus and dust from the nasal cavity into the throat, where they are swallowed. Most bacteria or other germs trapped in the mucus will be killed by the strong acid in your stomach (*see page 13*). You produce lots of mucus when you have a cold or the flu.

Larynx

Trachea

Cartilage

Cilia

Blood vessel

Muscles

Cartilage

THE TRACHEA
After it has traveled through the larynx the warmed, clean air reaches a tube called the trachea. The trachea is protected by about 20 C-shaped pieces of hard **cartilage**. You can feel them if you rub your hand gently up and down the front of your neck. They prevent the trachea from collapsing. The back of the trachea has no cartilage, only soft, muscle tissue which allows the trachea to bend as you move your head.

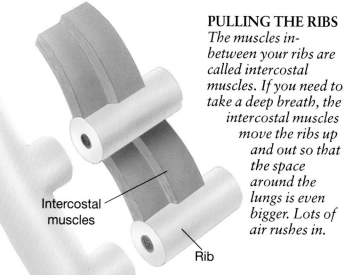

PULLING THE RIBS
The muscles in-between your ribs are called intercostal muscles. If you need to take a deep breath, the intercostal muscles move the ribs up and out so that the space around the lungs is even bigger. Lots of air rushes in.

Intercostal muscles

Rib

BREATHING FACTS
*If you eat or drink too quickly, or laugh too much, the diaphragm can start to contract in spasms. The space between the **vocal cords** closes and air is trapped. The air then rushes out in a loud hiccup.*

Before you cough, you take a really deep breath. The space between the vocal chords closes so the air cannot escape. Then the air rushes suddenly past the vocal chords making a loud noise and helping to clear the air passages.

Sneezing happens in the same way as coughing except that the air is forced to escape through your nose. This helps to clear your nose.

Inside the lungs

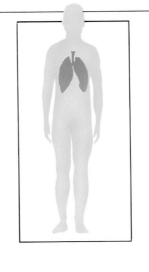

The respiratory system starts at the nose and mouth. The air then travels down the trachea towards the lungs. Each part of the respiratory system gets smaller and more delicate as the air gets closer to the blood. Breathing is only the first stage in a whole series of events called **respiration**. Once air has reached the lungs, oxygen passes into the bloodstream and is carried to all the cells in the body.

Trachea

The trachea branches into two smaller tubes called bronchi. These in turn branch into lots of smaller tubes, called bronchioles. They carry the air down to reach all parts of the lungs.

The bronchioles branch into very thin tubes, finer than a human hair. At the ends of these tubes are tiny air sacs, or alveoli. The alveoli have such thin walls that gases can easily pass through into the surrounding capillaries.

Bronchi

Capillaries

Alveolus

Oxygen

Alveolus

Carbon dioxide

Capillary

ALVEOLI

There are about 300 million alveoli in your lungs. They have a huge surface area to allow lots of oxygen from the air to come into contact with lots of blood in the capillaries during every breath. The outer surface of each alveolus is covered by tiny capillary blood vessels. The oxygen is transported around the body in the bloodstream. It is used to change food into energy. During this process a waste gas, carbon dioxide, is produced. The carbon dioxide moves back from the bloodstream to the alveoli in the lungs. Then it is breathed out through the nose and mouth.

During normal breathing about 500 cubic centimeters of air goes in and out of your lungs. When you are exercising you breathe lots more air in and out – about 3000 cubic centimeters. You can breathe out about 1600 cubic centimeters of air, but at least 1200 cubic centimeters will always remain inside.

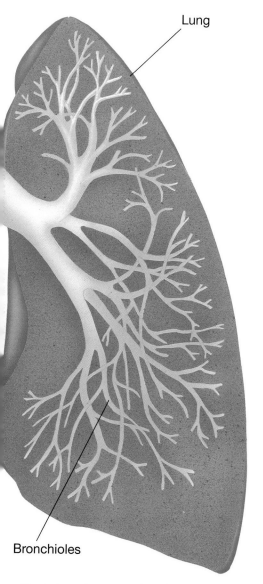

Lung

Bronchioles

Each lung is covered with special membranes, called pleura. Between the pleura is a layer of liquid which helps the lungs to move easily while you breathe. The right lung is larger than the left lung and is divided into three parts, called lobes, instead of the left lung's two.

LUNGS FACTS

Car fumes and cigarette smoke contain a poisonous gas called carbon monoxide. In large quantities, carbon monoxide could suffocate you. This is because it combines with the hemoglobin in the blood leaving no space for oxygen to be carried around the body.

When you feel out of breath while you are exercising it does not mean that you are not breathing in enough oxygen. It is more likely that your heart cannot pump the oxygenated blood around the body quickly enough.

If you spread all the alveoli in your lungs out flat they would have about the same surface area as a tennis court. If all the capillaries in the lungs were laid end to end they would reach almost from New York to London.

EXCHANGING GASES

When oxygen enters the bloodstream through the alveoli it dissolves in the liquid plasma in the blood and then joins to the hemoglobin molecule in the red blood cells. The blood flows around the body and the oxgen molecule breaks away and enters the muscle cells.

As blood moves through your muscle cells it picks up the waste gas, carbon dioxide. The carbon dioxide dissolves in the blood. When you exercise, your muscles produce lots of carbon dioxide and become very warm and acidic. This sends signals to the blood to release lots more oxygen into the muscle cells so that they can work harder.

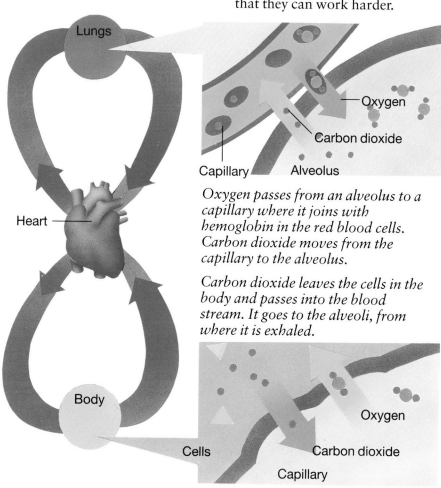

Lungs

Heart

Body

Oxygen

Carbon dioxide

Capillary   Alveolus

Oxygen passes from an alveolus to a capillary where it joins with hemoglobin in the red blood cells. Carbon dioxide moves from the capillary to the alveolus.

Carbon dioxide leaves the cells in the body and passes into the blood stream. It goes to the alveoli, from where it is exhaled.

Oxygen

Cells   Carbon dioxide

Capillary

The amazing brain

The brain is a very complicated organ that can handle thousands of pieces of information at the same time. It interprets and responds to messages from the nervous system around the body. Some parts of the brain allow you to learn new skills or think about difficult problems. Other parts deal with activities that you are not aware of, such as controlling your body temperature, breathing and your heartbeat.

The brain can be divided into three main areas. The largest area is the cerebrum which controls your language, reasoning and memory. The cerebellum sits at the back of the head and helps to co-ordinate muscle movements. The brain stem connects all the brain areas together.

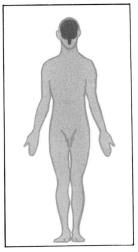

AREAS OF THE BRAIN
Each part of the cerebral cortext receives messages from a certain part of the body through the sensory nerves. When we see something, the information is processed in an area at the back of the cortex. Sounds are processed at the base of the cortex.

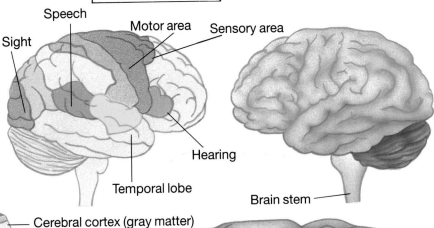

Speech

Sight

Motor area

Sensory area

Hearing

Temporal lobe

Brain stem

Cerebral cortex (gray matter)

Cerebrum

*Each half of the cerebrum has an outer layer of gray matter, called the **cerebral cortex**. It is covered in deep grooves and ridges like a walnut to give more surface area. The cerebral cortex is a solid mass of nerve fibers. These nerve fibers are called **neurons**. The neurons transmit messages at speeds of over 250 mph.*

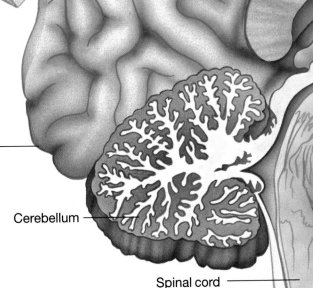

The cerebellum processes all the messages coming from the cerebral cortex concerned with body movements. It sends commands through the brain stem and **spinal cord**.

Cerebellum

Spinal cord

Hypothalamus

Pituitary gland

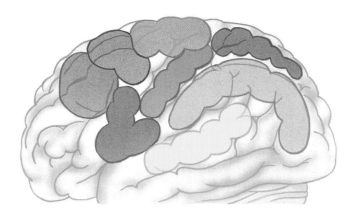

THOUGHT PROCESSES

Humans are capable of very complicated thoughts. When you are awake, you can work out problems, remember things from the past, make judgements and be happy, sad, angry or jealous. Most of these thought processes take place in the front of the brain.

THE MOTOR CORTEX

The motor cortex, in the middle of the cerebrum, sends out messages to control muscle movements all over the body.

At the base of the brain is the pituitary gland. It contains cells that produce many different chemicals called hormones. The pituitary hormones are carried around the body in the blood. They carry messages to make other glands produce their own hormones.

THE SENSORY CORTEX

Messages carrying information about feeling in different parts of the body are carried to the strip of cerebrum called the sensory cortex.

GLANDS AND HORMONES

Glands produce chemical messages called hormones. The thyroid gland produces hormones to control growth. Adrenal glands produce adrenalin when you are excited or afraid.

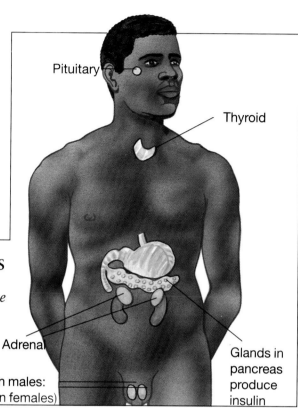

Pituitary

Thyroid

Adrenal

Testes (in males: ovaries in females)

Glands in pancreas produce insulin

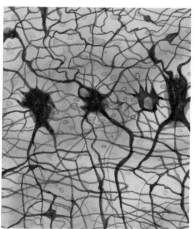

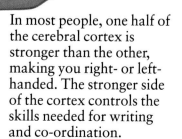

In most people, one half of the cerebral cortex is stronger than the other, making you right- or left-handed. The stronger side of the cortex controls the skills needed for writing and co-ordination.

NERVE PATHWAYS

Messages travel along the millions of nerve fibers in the brain like electrical signals in a circuit. They are directed along the right pathways by chemical 'switches' controlled by the cells in each neuron.

BRAIN FACTS

If the left side of your cerebral cortex is stronger then you will be right-handed. If the right side is stronger you will be left-handed. Only ten percent of people are left-handed. This means that the right hemisphere of the brain is usually stronger for reading, writing, speech and thought processes.

There are over one hundred billion neurons (or nerve cells) packed together in the brain.

Meningitis is a dangerous disease in which the membranes surrounding the brain become infected, causing the patient to have a very high temperature.

The human brain weighs over 3 lbs. This is about two percent of a person's total body weight.

Keeping in touch

Your body is a complicated machine made of hundreds of separate parts. To operate properly, all the parts must work together. The nervous system keeps all the parts of the body in touch with each other. The brain is the headquarters of the nervous system, receiving and sending messages. The nervous system allows you to control some functions, such as eating, while other functions, such as your heartbeat, happen automatically.

The nervous system is made up of millions of nerve cells, or neurons. Sensory neurons carry information about changes inside and outside the body to the brain and spinal cord. Motor neurons carry instructions from the brain and spinal cord to glands and muscles.

The nervous system is made up of the central nervous system – the brain and spinal cord – and the peripheral nervous system which connects the central nervous system to all other parts of the body. The central nervous system processes the nerve impulses sent from the rest of the body. The peripheral nervous system picks up information about changes outside the body.

Nerve impulses are a combination of chemical and electrical signals. They can travel at speeds of around 13 feet per second so that we can react to things almost instantly.

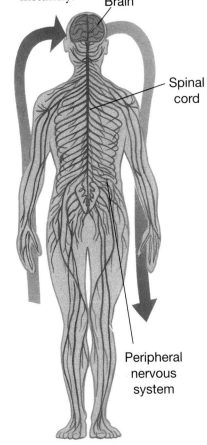

Brain

Spinal cord

Peripheral nervous system

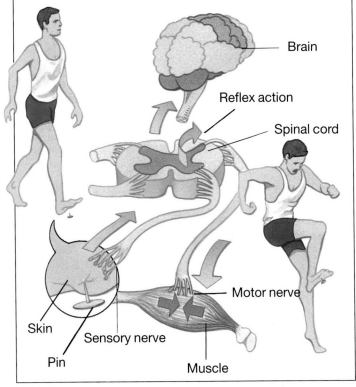

A REFLEX ARC
A reflex arc is a simple nerve pathway which allows you to react quickly to something. If you step on a drawing pin, a reflex arc comes into action. A pain receptor in your foot sends a message through the sensory nerve up your leg to the spinal cord. The motor nerve carries a signal back down to the leg to make your leg and foot muscles jerk upwards.

Brain

Reflex action

Spinal cord

Motor nerve

Skin

Sensory nerve

Pin

Muscle

THE SPINAL CORD
The spinal cord is a thick bundle of nerve tissue that comes directly from the brain. It is protected by bones in the spine called the vertebrae (*see page 9*). The spinal cord is divided into 31 sections, each with a pair of peripheral nerves branching out from it to either side of the body. All the sensory and motor nerves, except those in the head, meet at the spinal cord before passing on to the brain.

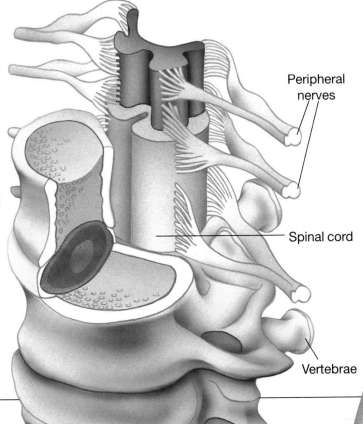

Peripheral nerves

Spinal cord

Vertebrae

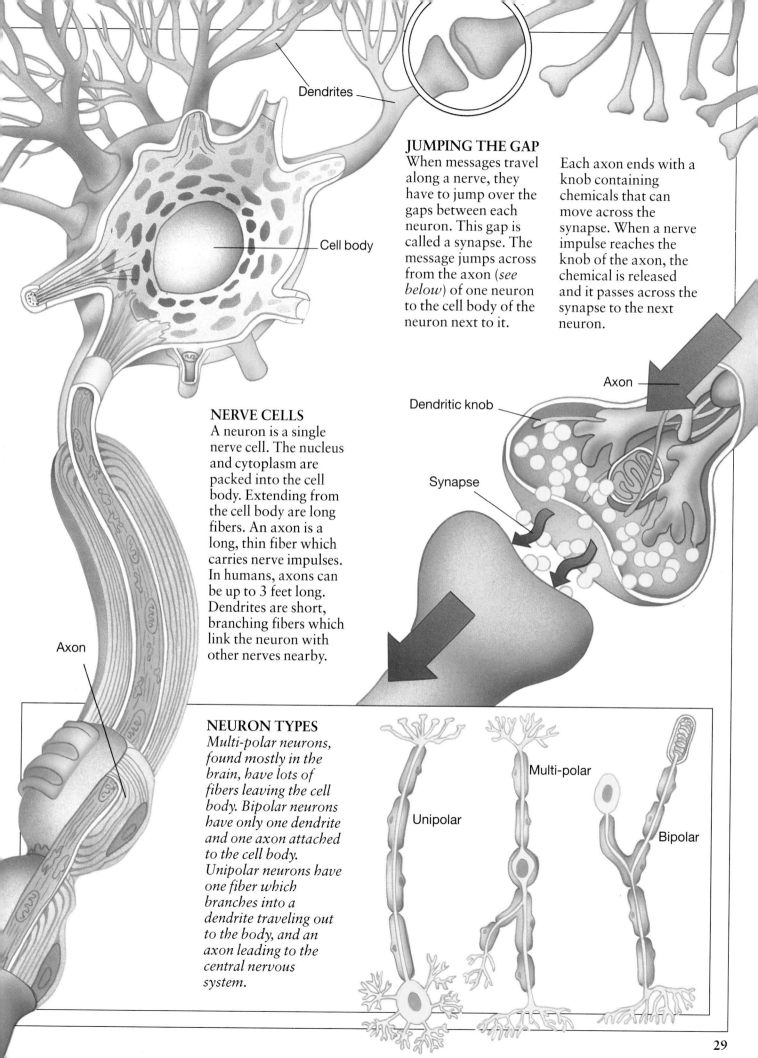

Dendrites

Cell body

JUMPING THE GAP
When messages travel along a nerve, they have to jump over the gaps between each neuron. This gap is called a synapse. The message jumps across from the axon (*see below*) of one neuron to the cell body of the neuron next to it.

Each axon ends with a knob containing chemicals that can move across the synapse. When a nerve impulse reaches the knob of the axon, the chemical is released and it passes across the synapse to the next neuron.

Axon

Dendritic knob

Synapse

NERVE CELLS
A neuron is a single nerve cell. The nucleus and cytoplasm are packed into the cell body. Extending from the cell body are long fibers. An axon is a long, thin fiber which carries nerve impulses. In humans, axons can be up to 3 feet long. Dendrites are short, branching fibers which link the neuron with other nerves nearby.

Axon

NEURON TYPES
Multi-polar neurons, found mostly in the brain, have lots of fibers leaving the cell body. Bipolar neurons have only one dendrite and one axon attached to the cell body. Unipolar neurons have one fiber which branches into a dendrite traveling out to the body, and an axon leading to the central nervous system.

Unipolar

Multi-polar

Bipolar

How do you feel?

Your body can sense changes in its surroundings. Your skin is in direct contact with the outside world, and it is here that most of the sensory receptors are found. The sensory receptors allow you to feel pain, heat, pressure and many other things. The top layer of skin is formed out of dead cells that protect the layers beneath. However, skin does not only protect – it also stores fat, gets rid of waste and helps to keep your body temperature constant.

The nerve sensors on the fingertips are particularly sensitive. There are hundreds of types of sensors, each covering the end of a sensory nerve fiber. When many of these sensors are triggered at the same time a strong message is sent down the nerve fiber to the brain.

Pressure receptors in the lower layers of the skin send messages to the brain when they sense heavy pressure on the surrounding tissue.

The nerves from the fingertips join up to form larger nerves that carry messages from the whole hand. In turn, these connect with other nerves as they travel up the arm towards spinal cord.

Special sensors in the skin are sensitive to changes such as hot and cold, rough and smooth. Each sensor is connected to a network of nerves which joins the central nervous system (*see page 28*). Messages from the sensors in the skin are sent along the spinal cord to the brain.

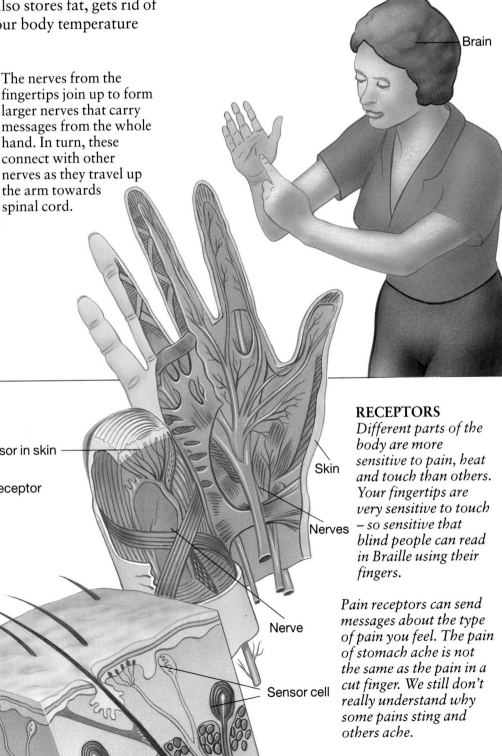

Brain

Sensor in skin

Pressure receptor

Nerve to brain

Skin

Nerves

Nerve

Sensor cell

RECEPTORS
Different parts of the body are more sensitive to pain, heat and touch than others. Your fingertips are very sensitive to touch – so sensitive that blind people can read in Braille using their fingers.

Pain receptors can send messages about the type of pain you feel. The pain of stomach ache is not the same as the pain in a cut finger. We still don't really understand why some pains sting and others ache.

SKIN LAYERS

The top layer of skin, the epidermis, is worn away every day as we move around. The epidermis is waterproof to stop water getting in and fluids getting out. The dermis lies underneath the epidermis. It is made up of layers of tough elastic fibers to make the skin strong, as well as blood vessels, nerve endings, hair **follicles** and sweat glands.

Hairs

Epidermis

Pore

Pore

Hair follicle

Hair erector muscle

Sweat gland

Coiled tube

Dermis

Subcutaneous layer

The subcutaneous layer is the bottom layer of the skin. This layer contains loose fatty tissue which helps to keep heat in. Elastic fibers run through the subcutaneous layer to connect the dermis to the muscle underneath.

GOOSE BUMPS

Muscle shortens

Muscle

Each hair in the skin is connected to a tiny muscle at its base. When you are cold, a nerve impulse is sent to the muscle which shortens to pull the hair up straight. The skin around each hair makes a small bump, or 'goose bump'.

SWEAT GLANDS

Each sweat gland has a coiled tube in the dermis, containing cells that make sweat. Heat causes the sweat to rise up the tube to the surface of the skin where it comes out through a tiny hole, or pore. As the sweat evaporates off your skin it makes you feel cooler.

SKIN SENSORS

The skin is full of special cells which can sense changes in the outside world. The skin sensors can detect heat, cold, pain, light touch and heavy touch, or pressure. Some sensor cells can only sense one kind of touch, others can sense more than one. The information they receive is sent to the brain through the nervous system to be processed.

Pain

Touch

Temperature

Pressure

Seeing things

Your eyes are the organs through which you see things and record the world around you. Each eye is about 1 inch across, and sits in a hole in the skull. At the front of the eye is a lens which focuses by being squeezed or extended. The iris controls the amount of light entering the lens. At the back of the eye, the retina is packed with nerves which are sensitive to light. The eyelids and lashes help to protect the eye.

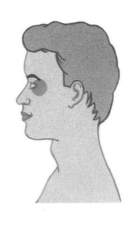

Light is collected by the lens at the front of the eye. The lens focuses the light so that a clear picture is formed on the retina at the back of the eye. The hundreds of images that enter the eye every second are edited by the brain to make a ontinuous sequence.

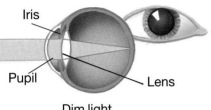

Iris

Pupil

Lens

Dim light

Iris

Pupil

Lens

Bright light

THE IRIS AND PUPIL
When you look at an eye, the colored center portion you can see is the iris. This is a ring of muscle. In bright light the iris makes the pupil smaller to allow less light to enter; in dim light the iris makes the pupil larger to enable more light to enter.

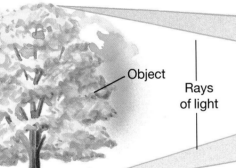

Object

Rays of light

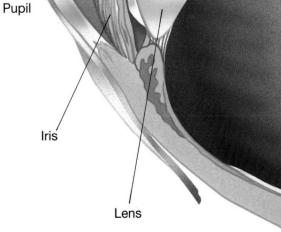

Pupil

Iris

Lens

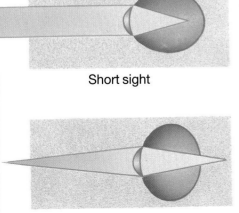

Short sight

Long sight

FAULTY VISION
In some people's eyes the lenses do not focus properly on objects at certain distances. People with short sight cannot focus distant objects on the retina. A **concave** lens in glasses will correct this. People with long sight cannot focus close objects. This is corrected by glasses with a **convex** lens.

32

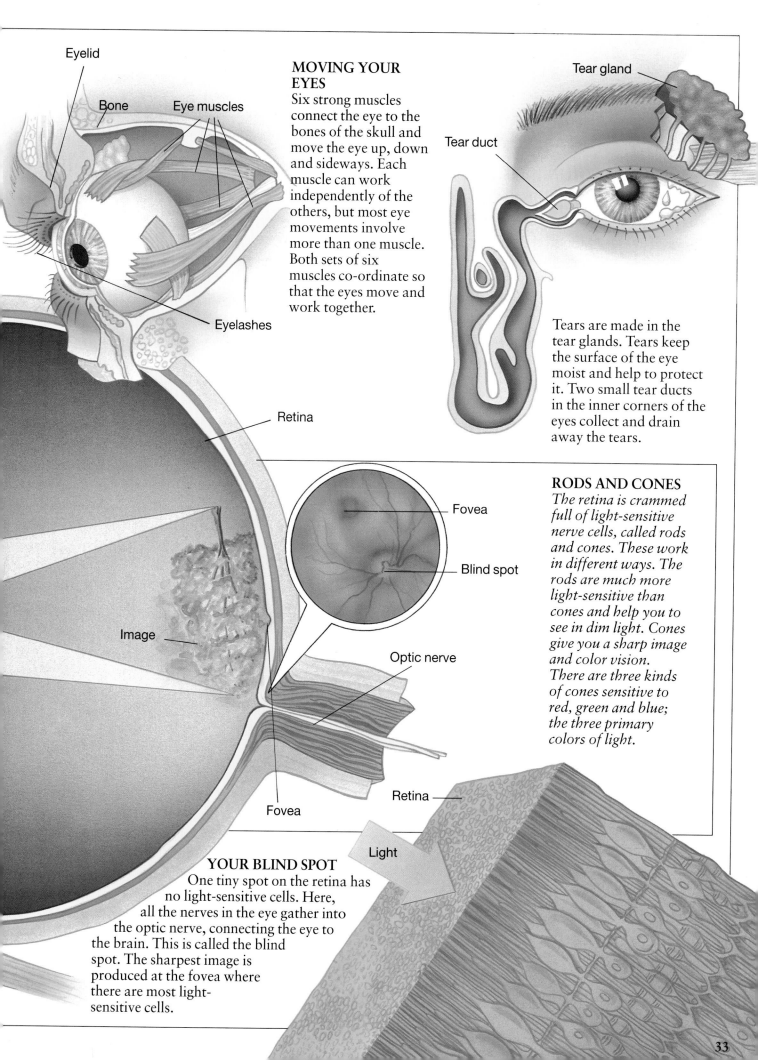

Eyelid

Bone   Eye muscles

Tear gland

MOVING YOUR EYES

Six strong muscles connect the eye to the bones of the skull and move the eye up, down and sideways. Each muscle can work independently of the others, but most eye movements involve more than one muscle. Both sets of six muscles co-ordinate so that the eyes move and work together.

Tear duct

Eyelashes

Retina

Tears are made in the tear glands. Tears keep the surface of the eye moist and help to protect it. Two small tear ducts in the inner corners of the eyes collect and drain away the tears.

Fovea

Blind spot

RODS AND CONES

The retina is crammed full of light-sensitive nerve cells, called rods and cones. These work in different ways. The rods are much more light-sensitive than cones and help you to see in dim light. Cones give you a sharp image and color vision. There are three kinds of cones sensitive to red, green and blue; the three primary colors of light.

Image

Optic nerve

Retina

Fovea

Light

YOUR BLIND SPOT

One tiny spot on the retina has no light-sensitive cells. Here, all the nerves in the eye gather into the optic nerve, connecting the eye to the brain. This is called the blind spot. The sharpest image is produced at the fovea where there are most light-sensitive cells.

Making sounds

Hearing is one of the ways that the body senses what is going on around it. You can sense danger, communicate and judge distances – all by listening. Your ears can detect sounds from the tinest whisper to the loudest machine. Although you hear lots of sounds, you only listen to some of them. The brain can interpret and recognize sounds, enabling you to listen out for certain sounds, such as voices, and to ignore others.

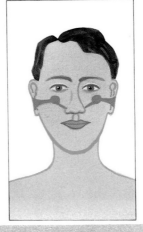

The sounds you hear are created when objects vibrate. The vibrations are carried through the air as sound waves. The outer ear picks up the sound waves and directs them down inside the ear. From here, the sound information is sent to your brain.

INSIDE THE EAR
The bit of your ear that sticks out is only a small part of the whole ear. The outer ear flap, called the pinna, collects and directs sound waves down your ear canal to the eardrum, stretched across the bottom of the ear canal.

Vibrations in the eardrum are passed on to three tiny bones, the tiniest in the whole body. They are called the hammer, anvil and stirrup. They form a bridge between the eardrum and the inner ear. The bones make the vibrations stronger before passing them on to the oval window.

The inner ear contains two sections. The cochlea contains the sensory cells that 'hear' the sound vibrations passing through from the middle ear. The semi-circular canals help you to keep your balance.

Inside the cochlea there are hundreds of hearing receptor cells covered in sensitive hairs. Above the hairs lies a membrane which receives sound vibrations and moves across the sensitive hairs. As it moves, it makes the hairs move in different directions. Each movement triggers a different nerve signal which can then be interpreted by the brain as distinct sounds.

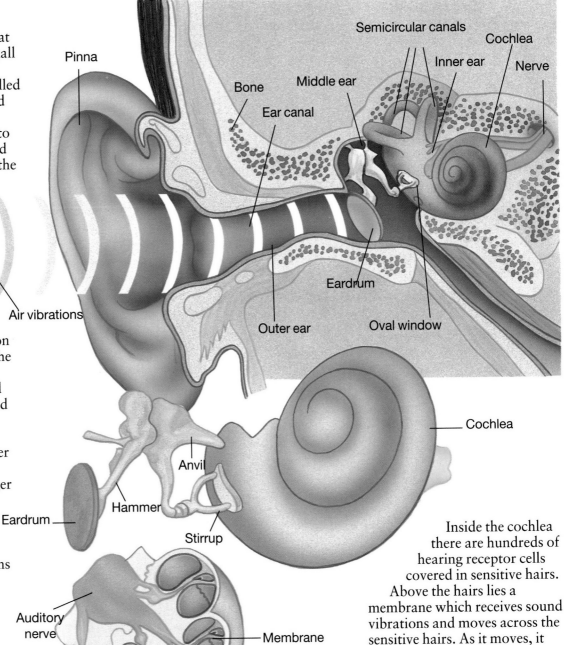

Pinna

Bone

Ear canal

Semicircular canals

Cochlea

Inner ear

Nerve

Middle ear

Eardrum

Air vibrations

Outer ear

Oval window

Cochlea

Anvil

Hammer

Eardrum

Stirrup

Auditory nerve

Membrane

Hairs

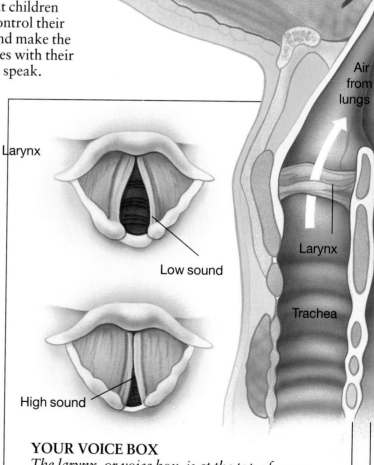

HEARING FACTS

The pitch of sound – how high or low it is – is measured in hertz (Hz). Your ears can hear sounds as low as 20 Hz, and as high as 20,000 Hz. Dogs can hear sounds that humans cannot hear because they are too high – up to 40,000 Hz.

There are about 25,000 tiny hair-like receptor cells in the cochlea of each ear.

The volume of sound – how quiet or loud it is – is measured in decibels (Db). Whispering is about 25 Db, normal conversations is about 50–60 Db. Noise over about 80 Db is dangerous for your ears.

If you spin round and round very fast the fluid in your semicircular canals picks up so much speed that it does not stop moving when you do. This is why you feel dizzy.

MAKING SOUNDS

The flaps of skin in the larynx, known as the vocal cords, vibrate if air is forced past them. The vibrations make sound waves that travel up your throat into the mouth. The sound waves are formed into words or sounds by changing the shape of your tongue and your lips. The tongue and lips have lots of small muscles which can help you to make very precise sounds. Humans makes some sounds naturally, for example the crying of babies, but children learn to control their tongues and make the right shapes with their mouths to speak.

Lips

Tongue

Air from lungs

Larynx

Trachea

THE SEMICIRCULAR CANALS

The semicircular canals are three delicate curved tubes filled with liquid. They lie at right angles to one another. Each canal has a small swelling called an ampulla which contains sensory hairs. However much you move your head about, the liquid in the canals always stays level. The movement of the liquid pulls on the hairs, and they send information to the brain so that you don't fall over.

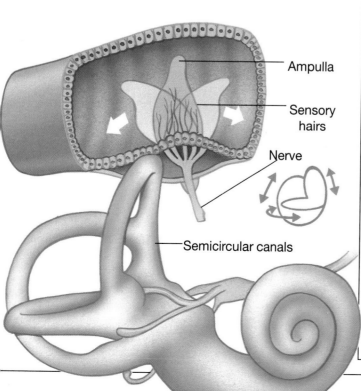

Ampulla

Sensory hairs

Nerve

Semicircular canals

Larynx

Low sound

High sound

YOUR VOICE BOX

The larynx, or voice box, is at the top of your trachea. It is made up of sheets of elastic fibers, muscle and cartilage. The lower folds of muscle are called the vocal cords. When they are open they make a triangular slit which allows air to pass through easily. The elastic fibers vibrate when air is forced past them and form sound waves.

Your sense of smell

There are five senses which give you information about your surroundings: sight, hearing, touch, smell and taste. Smell and taste are particularly closely linked. Both smell and taste react to chemical substances rather than vibrations like hearing, sight and touch. Smell and taste are important because they help you to recognize that what you are eating is not dangerous.

Even as babies, humans can tell which smells are nice and which are unpleasant. Nerve cells carry information to the brain from the olfactory cells. You learn from an early age that nasty smells are usually associated with things that are dangerous to eat.

At the top of each nostril are two small patches of nerve cells, called olfactory cells. These form the only part of the nose actively involved in smelling. The rest of the nose is used for warming and cleaning air.

Each nostril is lined with a layer of mucus and sensitive hairs. These hairs are the dendrites (*see page 29*) of the olfactory cells which lie at the top of the nostril.

Olfactory cells

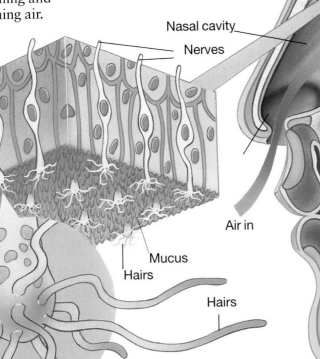

Nasal cavity

Nerves

Air in

Mucus

Hairs

Hairs

HAIRS IN THE NOSE
The olfactory cells have tiny hair-like cilia on their tips which stick out into the nostril. These sensitive hairs detect and label different smells. Each smell is a mixture of chemicals, carried as gases in the air. The cilia produce a sticky mucus which dissolves the chemical smell. We can probably recognize different smells because each chemical smell molecule has a particular shape which fits a particular sensory cell, rather like a jigsaw. The nerve cell reacts when the pieces fit.

Salty

Sweet

Sour

Bitter

BITTER AND SWEET
The tongue is covered with cells called taste buds. They can detect four basic tastes: sweet, sour, salty and bitter. Sweet tastes are detected at the very tip of the tongue. Sour tastes are recognized by the buds at the edges of the center of the tongue. The buds at the back pick up salty tastes, while at the very back of the tongue, buds detect bitter tastes. The tongue moves food around the mouth to identify all the flavors.

TASTE BUDS
Taste buds are tiny bundles of cells that lie underneath the surface of the tongue. Above them are small bumps which you can easily see on your tongue. Your mouth produces **saliva** which helps to dissolve the chemicals producing taste. These chemicals run down tiny holes in the bumps to reach the taste buds at the bottom. Each taste bud has a sensory nerve which takes the taste message to the brain.

Surface of tongue

Sensory of cells

Nerves to brain

Taste bud

Nerves to brain

As it moves around the mouth, the tongue pushes food towards the teeth to be chewed and crunched. Muscles help the tongue to move food in all directions. A thin layer of cells that coat the tongue contain the taste buds. The receptors in the taste buds also react to pain, which is why it hurts so much when your bite your tongue. The tongue is also important for speech. Its shape is altered to form recognizable sounds.

37

Bending and stretching

The skeleton is the structure that supports the whole body. It provides a strong framework for the soft organs and muscles in the body. The skeleton is made up of bones and joints that give both strength and flexibility at the same time. There are joints wherever two or more bones touch. The bones of the skeleton are linked with the nervous system and the muscles allow you to make controlled movements that can be small or forceful.

The femur is the longest bone in the body. It reaches from your hip to your knee. The top end of the femur is ball-shaped to fit snugly into the rounded socket of the hip joint, making a 'ball and socket' joint.

Compact bone

If you did not have bones in your body you would collapse like a rag doll. Bone is made up of proteins, living cells and minerals. Each bone in the body is like a tube. In the center is a soft substance called bone marrow which stores fat and produces new blood cells. Around this is a long tube made up of smooth, solid bone. The rounded ends of the bone are made of a lighter, spongy bone.

Bone

Spongy bone

The spongy tissue at the ends of the bone contains lots of bony plates which join together like a honeycomb with airspaces in-between. This makes the bone light but strong.

Compact bone

COMPACT BONE
The long tube of bone, called compact bone, is made up of a tough protein, called collagen, and minerals. The collagen and minerals are cemented together in a series of rings. In the center of each ring is a small channel called the Haversian canal. Each canal contains one or two small blood vessels which bring food to the bone cells.

Haversian canal

vessels

The living bone cells are found in tiny chambers in the canal system of the compact bone. In-between the cells, fibers of collagen make the bone strong and resistant to bumps.

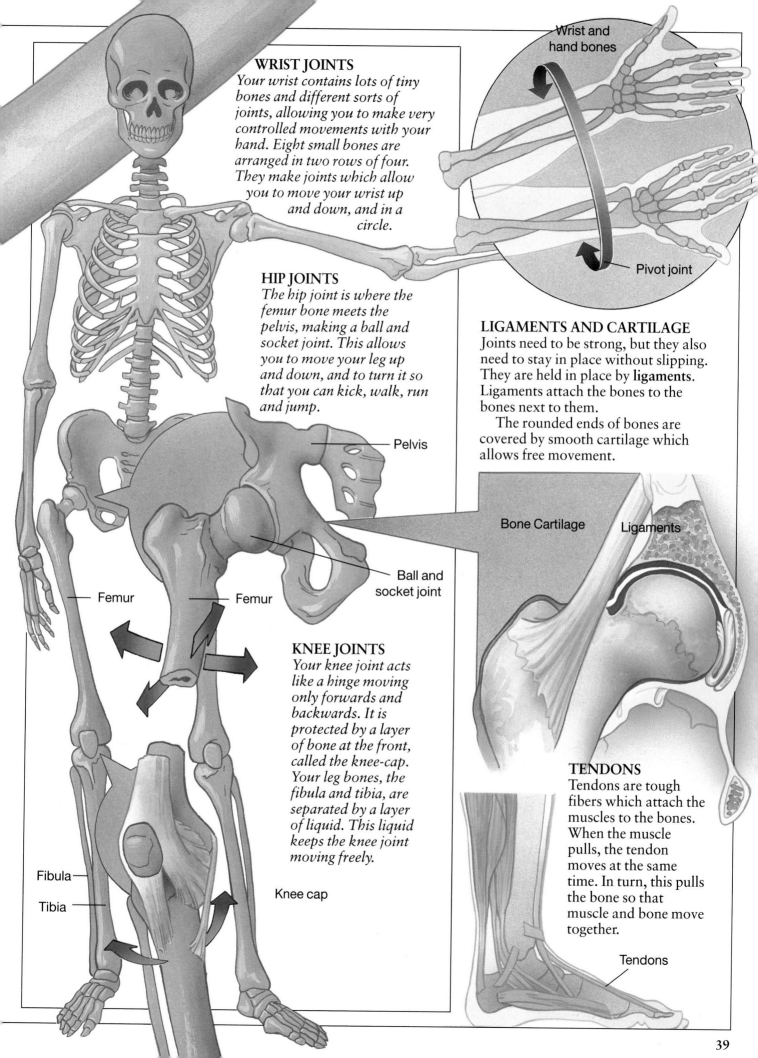

WRIST JOINTS
Your wrist contains lots of tiny bones and different sorts of joints, allowing you to make very controlled movements with your hand. Eight small bones are arranged in two rows of four. They make joints which allow you to move your wrist up and down, and in a circle.

Wrist and hand bones

Pivot joint

HIP JOINTS
The hip joint is where the femur bone meets the pelvis, making a ball and socket joint. This allows you to move your leg up and down, and to turn it so that you can kick, walk, run and jump.

Pelvis

Ball and socket joint

Femur

Femur

KNEE JOINTS
Your knee joint acts like a hinge moving only forwards and backwards. It is protected by a layer of bone at the front, called the knee-cap. Your leg bones, the fibula and tibia, are separated by a layer of liquid. This liquid keeps the knee joint moving freely.

Knee cap

Fibula

Tibia

LIGAMENTS AND CARTILAGE
Joints need to be strong, but they also need to stay in place without slipping. They are held in place by **ligaments**. Ligaments attach the bones to the bones next to them.

The rounded ends of bones are covered by smooth cartilage which allows free movement.

Bone Cartilage

Ligaments

TENDONS
Tendons are tough fibers which attach the muscles to the bones. When the muscle pulls, the tendon moves at the same time. In turn, this pulls the bone so that muscle and bone move together.

Tendons

Muscle power

Muscles make up a third of your body weight. There are over 650 muscles and they are found in every part of your body. Each muscle is made up of special cells which are usually long and thin. Muscles can change the energy from food into energy for movement. There are three types of muscle tissue – skeletal, smooth and cardiac. Most skeletal muscles are attached to bones.

Each muscle is covered with a fibrous tissue. This tissue keeps each muscle separate. The outer tissue stretches out into a tough cord called the tendon. The tendon attaches to the outer cover of the bone, or to other muscles. Some tendons are very long. For example, your fingers are moved by muscles in your arm. You can feel the tendons running along the back of your hand.

Each muscle is separated into bundles of fibers. The muscle fibers have a coat of thin protective tissue which connects all the bundles together.

You can train your muscles to work more efficiently by doing sport and exercise. Special exercises help you to develop stronger muscles in various parts of your body.

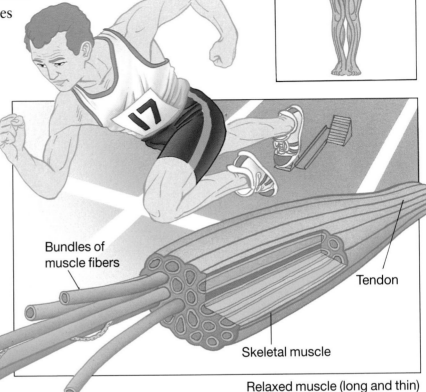

Bundles of muscle fibers

Tendon

Skeletal muscle

Relaxed muscle (long and thin)

Each fiber in the bundle is really a single muscle cell – a long, thin cylinder with rounded ends. The muscle cell has its own nucleus and lots of energy-packed mitochondria (*see page 10*). The fibers are sometimes as long as the whole muscle.

Muscle fibers

One muscle fiber

Actin filaments

Myosin filaments

The muscle fibers contain hundreds of smaller units, called myofibrils. The myofibrils stretch out along the muscle fiber. Myofibrils contain two types of tiny filaments, thick filaments and thin filaments. The filaments are made of different types of protein. These proteins make a pattern of dark and light stripes along the muscle fiber.

MUSCLE FACTS

Nearly all the muscles work in groups. When one muscle in the group contracts, another one will relax. You use six different muscles in your face every time you smile. These muscles help us to make lots of expressions.

Some of your muscles are working even when you appear to be resting or standing still. The reason why you fall over and collapse if you faint is because the muscles are no longer working to keep your upright.

DIFFERENT TYPES OF MUSCLE

Cardiac muscle is found in the heart. Smooth muscle is found in the iris of the eye, in blood vessels and in the gut. Smooth and cardiac muscles allow parts of the body to move without your having to think about it. This is why they continue to work while you sleep.

Cardiac muscle

Skeletal muscle

Smooth muscle

ACTIN AND MYOSIN

The protein filaments that make up the light stripes in the muscle fiber are called actin filaments. The darker stripes are called myosin filaments. Some of the actin filaments overlap with the myosin filaments. The myosin filaments have little attachments which can join to the actin filaments and pull them in so that they overlap even further. This is what makes the muscle contract, or shorten. When the filaments move apart again, the muscle relaxes. Not all the fibers in a muscle have to contract at the same time. This means that the pulling power of a muscle can vary.

Thin filaiments

Thick filaments

Contracted muscle (shorter and fatter)

Biceps relaxed

Triceps contracted

RELAXED MUSCLES

When your muscle is in a relaxed state, the actin and myosin filaments are spread out along the fiber and do not overlap very much. Muscles often work in pairs. When your arm is straight your biceps muscle is relaxed, and your triceps muscle is contracted.

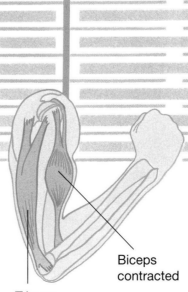

Biceps contracted

Triceps relaxed

CONTRACTED MUSCLES

When a muscle is sent a chemical signal from a nerve, it will contract. The actin and myosin filaments link together and slide closer to overlap. The muscle fiber gets shorter and thicker.

Getting Older

From the moment of birth you begin to age. Statistically women live longer than men, life expectancy for women in the developed world is 77, for men it is 73. The aging process is one of a progressive wearing out or failure of bodily functions. Cells consume less oxygen, divide more slowly and less accurately. Disease, poor environmental conditions and stress accelerate the aging process.

BIRTH
A new-born baby is too weak to support itself sitting upright. It can make grabbing movements and instinctively knows how to suck its mother's breast. It cannot focus its eye movements until about one month old.

PUBERTY
In girls, puberty – the start of sexual maturity – starts at around the age of 10 years, in boys it starts a year or two later. Both sexes start to grow pubic and underarm hair. A boy's sexual organs begin to grow and the voice 'breaks' or changes tone as the larynx grows. At around the age of 13 a girl's nipples darken and her period starts.

SITTING AND CRAWLING
A baby can begin to sit, if supported, at around the age of four months, and unaided at about six months. A baby can then reach for objects without tumbling over.

STANDING
Shortly after crawling a baby starts trying to pull itself up and lurch forward in a clumsy walking motion. Around its first birthday the first steps are often taken.

RUNNING
During the first year of life most babies learn to control their limbs. Not long before the second birthday most toddlers can run.

MATURITY
When young adults become emotionally mature they are ready to start their own family. If sexual intercourse takes place at the time when the female egg is mature, the woman may become pregnant and a new life cycle will begin.

Sitting

Crawling

Birth

Standing

Running

Maturity

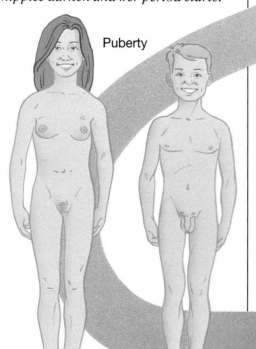

Puberty

BODY PROPORTIONS

At birth a baby's head is around one quarter of the total body length. Following the third birthday a child's body begins to catch up. Between the ages of 6 and 12 proportions stay the same until puberty begins.

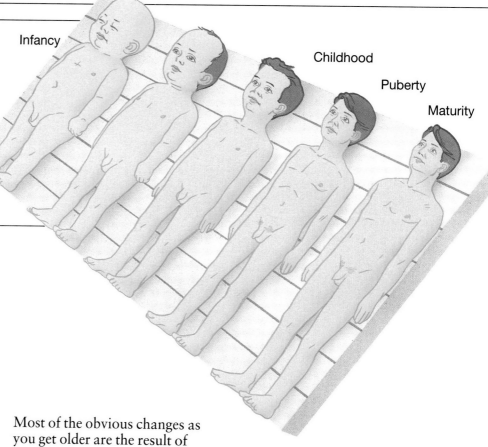

Infancy

Childhood

Puberty

Maturity

CELL LIFE

Some cells, such as skin cells, are continuously being replaced, but others live for many years. In early life all cells divide but as time passes and you become fully grown brain cells, nerve cells and muscle cells stop dividing and cannot be replaced if they die. Skin cells are continuously being shed as they come directly in contact with exterior influences. Every 19 days new skin cells are made.

Most of the obvious changes as you get older are the result of some kind of chemical or structural change in your body. Some cells and some substances stop being reproduced. For example, you will find that as you get older your skill will become less elastic. This is because the elastic tissue in your skin is not replaced properly after the age of about 30.

Scientists are constantly working to understand the aging process. Some believe that if the chemical processes involved in getting older can be understood, drugs can be developed to keep people alive much longer than now.

MENOPAUSE

Menopause generally occurs in women between the ages of 48 and 54. Their bodies stop producing a monthly egg and their periods cease.

OLD AGE

Old age is the final stage of life. Metabolism slows down and cells become less efficient. Older people find their joints can stiffen, making them less agile.

Glossary

amino acid The chemical building blocks of proteins.

antibody A chemical that helps the body to fight against infection by killing bacteria and viruses.

artery An elasticated tube that carries blood away from the heart.

bacteria Very small, single-celled organisms that live inside the body. Most bacteria are harmless and help the body to break down waste food material.

capillary One of the tiny tubes with extremely thin walls which carry blood through all the organs of the body.

carbohydrate Foods such as sugar and starch which provide lots of energy for the body.

cartilage Tough connective tissue that is made up of flexible fibers and rubbery gel. Cartilage helps to attach tendons to the bones of the skeleton.

cerebral cortex The outer layer of the front part of the brain. It has lots of folds and looks a bit like the surface of a walnut. It is the part of the brain involved in thinking and reasoning.

cholesterol A chemical found in some foods which is made up of white crystals. It can form a layer along the walls of the blood vessels, sometimes blocking them and causing heart disease.

concave The shape of a surface that curves inwards like a saucer.

convex The shape of a surface that curves outwards like the surface of an orange.

DNA Short for deoxyribonucleic acid. The complicated chemical 'ladder' that makes up the genetic material in your body.

energy The force that provides the power for work to be done. In the body cells this is through chemical or heat energy which is converted into movement in the muscles.

enzyme One of the special proteins that do important jobs in the body. Some enzymes help to digest food; others build new cells or help to control chemical reaction in the cells.

follicle The root of a body hair buried deep in your skin or scalp from which a hair will eventually grow.

gastric Anything to do with the stomach and digestive system.

genetic code Instructions in the form of strands of DNA found in the nucleus of each body cell.

gland A group of cells that produce special chemicals which have a certain job in the body.

glucose A simple type of sugar (made up of carbon, hydrogen and oxygen) which can be easily converted into energy for your body cells.

hemoglobin A chemical in the blood that carries oxygen around the body. It contains a central core of iron and gives blood its bright red color.

hormone A chemical messenger produced in clumps of cells called endocrine glands (for example, the thyroid gland).

hypothalamus The central part of the base of the brain. The hypothalamus is very important because it controls the nervous system and body temperature.

ligament A cord of fibrous tissue which binds two or more bones together at a joint.

lobe A sub-division of an organ such as the liver or lung.

lymph a colorless fluid containing mainly white blood cells, vital for attacking germs.

membrane A flexible sheet of tissue covering the surface of cells. It allows some substances to pass through it and keeps others out.

mineral A natural, inorganic substance such as calcium, phosphate and magnesium.

mucus A slimy liquid produced by cells in the nose, stomach and breathing passages which protects and lubricates.

nerve A bundle of fibers that carries messages in the form of electrical impulses between the brain, spinal cord and all other parts of the body.

neuron Neurons transmit electrical impulses and release chemicals that link up with other neurons.

nutrient A vital chemical substance which provides nourishment for the body.

organism A basic living structure.

pacemaker The nerve center in the heart that controls the beating of the heart.

pigment A substance that produces a certain color.

protein A chemical compound containing nitrogen that acts as food, essential for growth.

respiration The process in living organisms of taking in oxygen from the outside world and of returning waste carbon dioxide back to the air. The oxygen is 'burned' to provide energy.

spinal cord The thick cord of nerve tissue in the spine which connects the brain to the nerves of the body.

tissue A group of cells with a similar structure and function. Groups of tissue combine to form an organ.

urea One of the waste products made by the body is ammonia. The liver turns ammonia into urea. The urea is filtered out of the bloodstream by the kidneys and is taken out of the body in urine.

valve A device that controls the flow of a fluid. In a blood vessel the valve allows blood to flow in one direction only.

vein A thin-walled tube that carries blood towards the heart from the body tissues. The blood inside the veins is usually deoxygenated blood.

virus A tiny, simple organism that feeds and reproduces inside a cell and causes disease. The HIV virus is responsible for AIDS. Viruses cannot be killed by antibiotic medicines.

vitamin A chemical substance which is found in certain foods. Vitamins are essential for the body to work efficiently and stay healthy.

vocal cords Two pairs of folded membranes in the larynx. The vocal cords vibrate and produce sound when air is forced over them from the lungs.

water vapor Water in a gaseous state.

Index